In Loving Memory of the Most Endangered Species, the Black Male

– Volume I

AN ABSTRACT OF THE GOOD, THE BAD, & THE UGLY

Isis M. Elijah

Isis M. Elijah

The opinions expressed in this manuscript are solely the opinions of the author and do not represent the opinions or thoughts of the publisher. The author has represented and warranted full ownership and/or legal right to publish all the materials in this book.

In Loving Memory of the Most Endangered Species, the Black Male - Volume I
An Abstract of the Good, the Bad, and the Ugly
All Rights Reserved.
Copyright © 2013 Isis M. Elijah
v2.0

Cover Photo © 2013 JupiterImages Corporation. All rights reserved - used with permission.

This book may not be reproduced, transmitted, or stored in whole or in part by any means, including graphic, electronic, or mechanical without the express written consent of the publisher except in the case of brief quotations embodied in critical articles and reviews.

ISBN: 978-0-578-10358-7

Isis M. Elijah

PRINTED IN THE UNITED STATES OF AMERICA

DEDICATION

This book is dedicated to the families around the world that have lost their children, but especially their males. Males are beginning to lose sight of their true value and worth. Males carry on their family name. Males initiate reproduction. A true male presence is strong, firm, loving, and consistent. This true male presence is so desperately needed, wanted, and deserved.

I want to thank from the bottom of my heart God the Father, the Son, and the Holy Spirit. I want to thank my current pastor, our first lady, and my church family. Hey kiddo. I want to thank my entire family, and my dearest grandmother Millie (the love of my life). I want to thank one of my best friends, and her entire family (especially her four little angels). They invited me to every play, and I have yet to miss one. I want to thank everyone in Northeast Ohio for their continued support.

INTRODUCTION

The author, Isis M. Elijah, was raised in the southern town of Tuskegee, Alabama. When she became a teen she moved to Akron, Ohio (where she currently resides).

As a youth Isis worked several newspaper routes, played softball, but mostly kept to herself. When she does something she likes, she doesn't consider it work. She has found writing this book of poetry to be a passionate, yet meditating experience. This collective body of work encompasses her perception, and her authentic expression of poetry in abstract form.

Isis' poetry is her testimony, it is her story, and it is her song. She thinks of herself as a humming bird, and poetry is her only song to sing. It is the author's hope that her reader's feel her passion for life, and her love for people via these poems. These words just may save or positively influence someone's life.

Isis spent an entire decade leading, directing, and mentoring youth & young adults. In 2010 she received the Woman of the Year award from her previous church and pastor. This award was for volunteerism, hard work, and dedication to young people. In the past Isis worked hard to expose inner city youth to various empowerment & confidence building exercises such as public speaking, choir, and dance. She also worked along with community leaders in sponsoring various youth outreach programs. Some of the things these young people were exposed to were poetry slams, etiquette training classes, charitable fundraising, visiting the elderly, confidence building endeavors, trips, and empowerment forums that young people successfully lead.

CONTENTS

A Grain of Salt. 1
Surroundings. 2
Loving 3
Do Not Ask Me to Speak in Public 4
Helping Hands. 5
Drill 6
Has Anyone Seen My Keys? 7
Railroads, Bridges, Oceans, and Tunnels 8
Teary-Eyed 9
Eye of the Tiger 10
Bi? Are You Sure? If So, Then Soar 11
Senses 12
Our Children. 13
Have Mercy 14
The One 16
Quiet is Kept, You're Prejudiced 18
Tap In To Yourself 19
Butterflies 20
Friendship is Free 21
All of Us Have Bias 22
My Soul Mate 23
The Game Is On. 24
Today. 26
Better to Give Than to Receive, Sometimes 27
Can't 28
Voids 29
The Congregation 30
Blame it on the Distractions 32

Up the River Without a Hope	33
Lazy	34
Questions	35
Lonely	36
He Is Smelling Himself	37
Bad Day So Work It Out	38
One-Sided	40
Broken Heart	41
If There Is a God	42
Black on Black	43
Testimony	44
Leave	45
The "N" Word	47
Snakes	48
Witches	49
Is It Genocide or Homicide?	50
Eulogy for Slavery in the 21st Century	51
When Crazy Meets Crazy	53
Shade Tree	54
Y'All Breaking My Heart	55
Secret	56
Bring It Back	57
Dung	58

MOST ENDANGERED SPECIES

A GRAIN OF SALT

If your heart trembles when you speak, and you get nervous
Stop trying to hinder the pitter-patter
Embrace it and be moved
For you are love

ISIS M. ELIJAH

SURROUNDINGS

Are you uncomfortable in your surroundings?
Then wait
Do you smell fear?
Is it hate?
He's sending in his troops
Remain calm and undertone
Are you simply misunderstood, simply being yourself?
Full of self-pride
In like of the cards that have been dealt
Positive, confident, and sure
So why are you uncomfortable in your surroundings?
Loving the mate, job, and home
You got that promotion
But something feels wrong
Still uncomfortable in your surroundings
Stay cautious, and cloaked
You're not alone
Do the homework
Doors will open soon
Along with the fortune
Let your enemies destroy themselves
Thank you for the mighty blessing
Loving self, this time hit a home run
Now, be comfortable in your surroundings

MOST ENDANGERED SPECIES

LOVING

Scorned
Rough around the edges
Fears
Sensitivity
Hard
Guard up
Strong sexual desires must be satisfied
Short temper
Met with attention to detail
Insecurity
Met with stability
Lashing out
Met with a firm standing
Loving
Sweet
Loving

ISIS M. ELIJAH

DO NOT ASK ME TO SPEAK IN PUBLIC

Do not ask me to speak in public
For I may get emotional
Sometimes I sit in the back and act unsociable
I study my peers
Not always close to them
I am a passionate person
Sometimes distant
However, I love all people
But, when I speak in public
I get nervous
My voice trembles
I eat a peppermint
Smile
Inhale
Exhale
We are all equals
Release

HELPING HANDS

It has always been my desire
To be healthy, wealthy, happy, and wise
But in doing so
Not to cheat, steal, or beg
As long as I am allowed to have
Good health, strength, and knowledge

It is my duty to be self-sufficient
When I satisfy my needs
And some of my wants
It is my duty to help those
That cannot help themselves

ISIS M. ELIJAH

DRILL

Listen
Do not run away
Silence the noise-maker
Pay for the dwelling
Protect the temple

MOST ENDANGERED SPECIES

HAS ANYONE SEEN MY KEYS?

Life
Breath
Longevity
Prosperity
Wealth
Clothes
Social Consciousness
Children
Food
Shelter
Survival
Dream
Happiness
Love
Chase
Thrill

ISIS M. ELIJAH

RAILROADS, BRIDGES, OCEANS, AND TUNNELS

Will we ever know our ancestors?
Is there any harm?
In knowing whence we came
In initiating real healing and embrace
Genocide is still prevalent today
Just in a different way
The world is still filled with grief
Lifetimes in prison
For legal and illegal occupations
Vacations, homes, and cars for some
Modern-day slave
Spending hours on the block grinding
For what?
Someone's high to unreality
There is no value in Africa
Really
A joke
The place where everything was birthed
What pipe did you smoke?
So many different nationalities enslaved
Even today that still hasn't changed
Some thought that they would never see the day
And many did not
Since we are all in this big melting pot
When do we start the real loving and healing?

TEARY-EYED

When I was younger
I used to get upset
Angry with myself
For crying all the time
But as I got older
I learned to embrace that emotion
Learned that I have a passion for people
Learned that I have a heart
So as I grow to know
And love myself more
I've learned to listen to that crying emotion
And pay close attention, good or bad
To those that draw my tears

ISIS M. ELIJAH

EYE OF THE TIGER

That look so mean
Those ribs so lean
Honest never green
Beastly and confident
Dominant and ever-present
The way you look at me exudes confidence
Brings chills to my mind, body, and spirit
So warm and peaceful

IN LOVING MEMORY

BI? ARE YOU SURE?
IF SO, THEN SOAR

So you decided to keep it close
Then come on out
Brag and boast
Have you not made yourself aware?
Couldn't get a date of the opposite sex?
So you decided to change the pace
But are you happy?
Don't settle, no matter who you are
Have you considered all the options?
Is your like in hopes of not being lonely?-
Or is it simply curiosity?
If you are bi because you are sure
Then soar
But if you are on autopilot, then wake up
Losing yourself might cost you
Stay true to self
Self-love, always

ISIS M. ELIJAH

SENSES

How can you recognize the unfamiliar?
Something you do not know
Cloudy to sunlight
Darkness to light
Draw in
Blow out
Clear
Did you realize they were there?
Some people have to buy them

MOST ENDANGERED SPECIES
OUR CHILDREN

Let us put them first
Let us educate, educate, and educate them
Discipline them
Instill the best we have to offer in them
Be good parents, neighbors, and friends
Give them love
Attention
Firmness
Protection
Let us not enable them
Let us teach them to be self-sufficient
Reliable
Trustworthy
Honest
For they are our future
Beautiful children, it is up to you
To protect this great country we have left you
Make it better
For your children and grandchildren

ISIS M. ELIJAH

HAVE MERCY

Woke up this morning
Sick
Tired
Hurt
Legs won't move
Please pull me out of this bed
I need a little light
Help
Stop the kids from crying
Stop the phone from ringing
People I don't know
People I don't want to talk to
Why are they calling and bugging me?
Where are all the positive people?
Where are the people that want something out of life?
Tired of being around people
Not wanting anything

Please remove these green-eyed haters out of my life
Please help me bridge my own positive circle
Bless me
Love you
Thank you
I got up
I got out
Toil
No complaints

IN LOVING MEMORY

Not tired, weak, or weary

Love
Thank you for having grace and mercy on me

ISIS M. ELIJAH

THE ONE

Searching for the one
What if he never comes?
Where is my soul mate?
I deserve one
Spread thin
Cheated when courting many
Lonely when courting none
Searching and searching
Where is my love?
I can't choose anymore
I leave it all up to you
Some are married posing as single
Some are closet posing as straight
There are still people that believe in marriage
Even gays
There are still people that believe in loving
And being with only one at a time
Where are they?
Where is mine?
Am I too old-fashioned?
Will I ever have a love of my own?
Not just anything or anyone
I am the ISH!
Give me my own gentle person
Show me the one
'Cause what's in front of me is not it
Thanks for allowing me to back away from that old pit
Open the blinds

IN LOVING MEMORY

Answer the phone
Deciphered the code
My new man done even took out the garbage
He pays the bills
He is gentle, loving, and kind
Careful, he just might be the one

ISIS M. ELIJAH

QUIET IS KEPT, YOU'RE PREJUDICED

How many friends do you have of the opposite race?
How many of them do you allow up in your space?
How many do you invite to your family functions?
How many do you talk about or treat rambunctious?
How many do you talk about behind their backs?
How many have you been seen with out in public?
How many would you tell your child not to date?
Do not bring them home
That is not your preference
Your preference is a prejudice

TAP IN TO YOURSELF

Trying to find myself
Pain, heartache, sexy, handsome, bad, and good
Thoughtful, kind, strong, and witty
Everyone gets lonely sometimes
Open a good book
Pour a good glass of wine
Stop soul searching
Pure
Everyone is missing something
Do not question
Use that tragedy to make you stronger
That's your testimony
Overcame
Successful
Present in your child's life
Married your bride
Misery is not your life
A real man
Stand tall and poised
For it is a bastard that sows a seed and leaves
Build your blueprint
However you like, king
You are not a bastard
You are a MASTER

ISIS M. ELIJAH

BUTTERFLIES

I hope I always get butterflies
To me they represent passion
So many of them in succession
For I know when I speak it is heartfelt
The trembling, the heart-racing nervousness
Hyper and eager
But focused, poised, certain, and confident
I welcome the butterflies
Public speaking has never been my forte
As long as there is a positive message
That may help another, I say
Bring butterflies
As I speak they soon go away
When I feel my words
Out they spray
They only last for a short time anyway
As I take my seat
It is all over
There went my butterflies today
For I am certain they will appear again

FRIENDSHIP IS FREE

Gifts are nice gestures
Money is better
Cards are thoughtful
So are letters
I appreciate you and your simple kindness
Be my rock
And I will be yours
Let me lean on you
And I will be your sword
Be my friend
And you will never question my loyalty
Let me talk to you
And I will rock you to sleep
Talk to me
I will hear you
Be there for me
I will never leave you
I appreciate gifts, cards, and money
But those things can never replace your friendship

ISIS M. ELIJAH

ALL OF US HAVE BIAS

Everyone is biased
Or shall I say prejudiced
Yes, you and me
But let me try to understand your sensitivity
What name do you dislike?
What skin tone and why?
Did someone like me, ever scar you?
Mistreat you
Beat you
Is there any way I can reassure you?
Will you allow me to understand your sensitivity?

Will you in turn try to understand mine?
After you get to know me
Will you not cross that line?
Can you love me and I you?
Sincerely and respectfully
Do not play with me
I love you
Let me love you
And you love me
Respect me
Respectfully
Sincerely

MY SOUL MATE

I have been waiting for you all of my life
Thank you for sending me my soul mate
Exactly what I needed
I will never put him before my redeemer
Not sure how long I am allowed to have you
But I will love you for as long as I am allowed

ISIS M. ELIJAH

THE GAME IS ON

Aren't we hyper, excited, athletic, and energetic people?
Aren't we willing to work hard, and go the extra mile for games?
Don't we like the best?
Don't we like the best seats?
Floor seats, club seats
Loge accommodations
Life is the biggest event there is
Is it a game?
But there are also bench warmers in games, right?
Everyone can't start, right?
Some bench warmers play important roles, don't they?
The good bench warmers
Watch, study, and cheer on their teammates
They support them, train, and prepare themselves
For their opportunity to play
Some bench warmers are happy
Just to say they're on the same team
Is life a game when so many are apparently losing?
Isn't life a game?
So many of us feel
We can have our cake and eat it too
Don't we feel like we can mess our lives up today?-
And seek God tomorrow? God is forgiving, isn't He?
God is trusting, God is almighty
God can do anything
And once I am done throwing my life away
And once I am done doing drugs
And being promiscuous

IN LOVING MEMORY

And once I have found my husband
Or once I have found my wife
And once I have made my fortune
Once I have completed all of my goals
It won't be too late to seek God, will it?
The game is on
What position are you playing?
Or are you just being played?

ISIS M. ELIJAH

TODAY

Is it sunny or blue?
Is it hazy or hue?
Or is it crisp with a splash of dew?
For there is nothing like the smell, and scent of today

IN LOVING MEMORY

BETTER TO GIVE THAN TO RECEIVE, SOMETIMES

Better to give than to receive
I do believe
But when constant takers and beggars
Never return favors
Not going to be an enabler
Love helping those that help themselves
But please send the lazies to someone else

ISIS M. ELIJAH

CAN'T

If you tell me I cannot
I will
If you tell me no
I will find someone who will tell me yes
I will turn a negative
Into a positive
I will turn a curse against me
Right back at you
And I will make sure I am blessed
In the process

VOIDS

Voids need to be filled
Like bills need to be paid
Wake up
Ahhh voids
Extreme mind-blowing
Shock value
Shock culture
Latch key
Ignorance
Depression
Homelessness
Darkness
Extracurricular
Broken transportation
Poverty
Your mind has been blown
All alone
Trying to fill a void

ISIS M. ELIJAH

THE CONGREGATION

As we get comfortable and wiggle in our seats
Take off our coats, and acknowledge our brethren
Greet our visitors, and smile
Yes, we are at home, no worries, no doubts
Life is good for the congregation
Things are the same, familiar
We like it that way
We don't need to change
They are growing down the street
They are building senior homes
They are doing well for the community
So what, who cares?
We aren't doing anything wrong
What is their angle?
We are confident and strong
No slander, no corruption, no scandal here
We like it that way
We like it here
There's no need to change
Growth will eventually come and stay
They are growing down the street
They have two sermons on Sunday
That's only their beginning
We aren't losing souls
We don't have to rally in the streets
We don't have to be efficient about our time and money
Even though our ends don't meet
So what if we are wasteful?

IN LOVING MEMORY

There are more people across the street on the basketball court
Than in our congregation
Let's not change a thing
They all had better move to our swing
Let's not change a thing
We are comfortable here
Haven't you heard a thing?

ISIS M. ELIJAH

BLAME IT ON THE DISTRACTIONS

Is it him or her?
Must I suffer?
Longing for companionship
My mind often wonders
Why am I alone?
What am I doing wrong?
Who is my sweetie with?
Too much dismay
My mind often wonders
How can I help others?
Over-extending myself
I have nothing left
What am I going to do?
Now my bills are overdue
I can't seem to get ahead
Can't seem to get anything done
Finding ways to waste my time
Looking for excuses for not accomplishing goals
Worrying about things someone else is handling
Do all that I can
Stop worrying about the rest
Stop blaming it on the distractions

UP THE RIVER WITHOUT A HOPE

How can I when it don't?
How can I when you won't?
How can it ever reach the top?
In the bottom of a puddle of rocks
How can I ever be truthful?
'Cause when I do you take advantage
Too many bent on drama
Something's missing
Only do what you know how
Only do what you're taught
Struggling
Where is the sense of hope?
One day hopefully it will come
This race is too long
Too many have run and lost
So many have paid the ultimate cost
Will I ever cross the finish line?
There goes my sense of hope
Down the river with the last boat

ISIS M. ELIJAH

LAZY

Why are you so lazy?
Who do you think you are fooling?
Having fun losing?
You are not getting over on the system
Conjuring up an illness
That check is not yours
It belongs to those who need it
Seriously
Robbing the hood?
Sleeping your life away
Hurting your self-esteem
Envying hard-working people
Attempting to crush dreams
Stop being the problem
Find a solution
Love yourself and give yourself a new life
Yes, it is hard
Some make it look easy
Do what you have to do to get off the couch
Cry in the dark
Play your favorite music
Get your mind right
Dust yourself off
Get your energy back
Not a prescription
Hopefully loved ones are not watching you be lazy

QUESTIONS

Why are you asking me so many questions?
I've just met you
I don't know you
Exactly what is it that you do?
How much money do I make?
What is the name of the person I date?
Don't you think that is rather personal?
Where do I live?
Who is my family?
Do you ask because you simply want to know?
Or are you simply nosey?
Sometimes it is best to stop, watch, look, and see
Instead of asking so many questions about me
If you take the time to get to know me
You'll find out everything you want to know
Keep asking me so many questions
And I'll tell you nothing
Maybe make up something
Do you mean to harm me?
Do you mean to betray me?
What is your angle?
Don't worry
I won't keep you around long enough to find out

ISIS M. ELIJAH

LONELY

Another lonely day
Trying to be celibate
Flesh is what I seek
The comforts of real heat
Trying to be strong, not weak
Been here before
Not another loser
Better than this
Liars go away
Should I get a puppy?
It would keep me company
I need someone, something
Loving
Caring
Sharing
Smart
Strong
Determined
Faithful
That handles the business
Tired
Weak
Abandoned
Lonely

MOST ENDANGERED SPECIES

HE IS SMELLING HIMSELF

Ah, he is so cute
He is adorable
A good little boy, so sweet and handsome
Growing day by day
Into an awesome young dude
Until puberty sets in
Why are you acting so rude?
You know better
You were taught better than this
Why are you acting this way?
Have you gone mad?
Not your teen
Right
Oh no, not you
As he grows older
It will be your turn soon
Well, you just wait
I'll pencil you in

ISIS M. ELIJAH

BAD DAY SO WORK IT OUT

On my job it's like
A good bridge in the sky
Benefits and wages are both okay
Get in and get out
Just put in my eight
No taking it home
Got enough on the plate
Here come the politics
The office antics
I'm a leader, and a loner
If it's not positive
I'd rather leave it
Let's be friends, you say
Sure, but without the drama
Will not argue here
Not when it affects my money
So, if that's what you're on
I'll stand over here alone
Judged by peers
Everyone's struggle is different
Everyone's growth is not the same
Dare to be a renegade
No need to whisper and talk about me
If so, we can't be friends
Hopefully one day you'll see
Don't attempt to pass your fears & shortcomings off on me
My reflection is great

IN LOVING MEMORY

I like what I see
Looking back at me
Working diligently
To amplify my reflection

ISIS M. ELIJAH

ONE-SIDED

Tired of the one-sided
Always you and no me
Always give and no receive
Take, take, and take
I want to be free
No love, only regret
No remorse, no respect
Tired of the one-sided
And so I draw the line
I don't mind helping
But baby, I am not buying
Can I borrow some cash?
Can I borrow a quarter?
When I am in a pinch
Make that two quarters
Can I get fifty cents?
Can I call in an emergency?
Will you help me out of a cinch?
If the answer is no
Then, I don't need your half
Because you're half plus zero equals half, not whole

BROKEN HEART

Gentle and passive
Here is my hand
Extended to you
Exchange it with yours
Here is my graciousness
Why do you intend to take away my soul?
My heart is not gone
Your plot failed
The things you have not given me
You cannot take away
Your cup will remain empty
When your mission is to deceive
There is pain in your eyes
There is sickness and disease
Poison in your mind and heart
Self-destructive
No one can ever feel or know your pain
How does one stop this vicious cycle?
Take back your life
Start making good choices
Take time to mend yourself
And your broken heart

ISIS M. ELIJAH

IF THERE IS A GOD

Where is He?
Does God exist?
He does not love me
He would not allow his people to suffer
If He knows all
Why doesn't He hear my cry?
So much sin
Why doesn't God strike down my enemies?
Children starving
People homeless
Riddled with disease
No one loves me
My father does not claim me
While my mother sleeps with many men
And women
Where is the reward for doing well?
I want mine now
Just like everyone else

MOST ENDANGERED SPECIES

BLACK ON BLACK

Black on black
Is where it's at
But so is loving all mankind
With an open mind

ISIS M. ELIJAH

TESTIMONY

Ever been saved from something?
Was it something that couldn't be explained?
Got the hair done
Instead of paying bills
Tricking
Is it always someone else's fault?
Never blaming self
Bought that lobster dinner
Instead of tuna fish
Bought my sweetie rims
Instead of food for the kids
Impressing others
Instead of handling my own
Maybe I should stay at home sometimes
Maybe that is why it's called home
It costs to run the streets
So go ahead and roam
Life is full of choices
So preserve yourself
Once you get your life back
Share your testimony

LEAVE

Not bound
Not tied
Dysfunction
Instability
Never look back
Shame
No lights
No water
No heat
No shelter
No hair
No shoes on your feet
Vices
Mistreatment
Scorned
Manhood destroyed
Womanhood nonexistent
Leave
Leave the environment that bores this extreme
And don't take the problem with you
Sometimes the problem lies within you
Leave the problem
And birth the solution
There is a difference between running away and leaving
When you run away you house the same mess
When you leave you shed that mess

ISIS M. ELIJAH

And grow new flesh
Leave
Right now
Just leave

THE "N" WORD

The "N" word is dead
Now cut off its head
Freedom of speech exists
Are we a bunch of idiots?
Blacks don't own the word, no one does
Anyone can use it
Haven't you heard?
If someone other than a black person
Says the "N" word, is it okay?
Absolutely not
But we continue to slay ourselves anyway
Very simple, not complex
No need for media hype or a panel fix
Oh yes, blacks say it in a loving way
Surely our ancestors are turning in their graves
Seen the pictures of the nooses, hangings, burnings, and white sheets
The "N" word will never be a term of endearment
We own it now, we took it back
Isn't that a bunch of crap?
Think you can pick and choose a word to use
And exclude it from the rest of the world
Yeah, right
Tell us something long enough and we start to believe it
Believe you are a "N" if you want to
And you have been brainwashed and defeated

ISIS M. ELIJAH

SNAKES

If it wiggles, swags, and coils
Is it a snake?
Will you wait until it bites, before you inspect?
Will you allow it to poison you?
Does it enter your dreams at night?
What if it stands upright?
Can it still be a snake?
Does it haunt you?
Then step on it

MOST ENDANGERED SPECIES

WITCHES

Have you ever met a witch?
It's okay to substitute the first letter in witch
A male or female passing themselves off as bliss
Sweeter than sweet
Loving as ever
Can do no wrong
So you think
Will not harm another
Yes, very clever
Have you ever met a witch?
Someone that gives and gives
Never asking for anything in return
Yet buttering you up for the next big catch
Making sure they give you everything
To ensure they take everything
Have you ever met a witch?
And you finally woke up
Only to find that witch was an exorcist
Where is that pot of hot grits?

ISIS M. ELIJAH

IS IT GENOCIDE OR HOMICIDE?

Is it genocide or homicide?
Who died?
Who was it?
Brother
Father
Mother
Sister
Uncle
Or cousin
Who pulled the trigger?
Was it dealing or stealing?
Was the cause poverty, hunger, grief, or strife?
What was the weapon?
Was it a gun or a knife?
Maybe it was drugs or AIDS
It continues to spray
Bang, bang, who shot ya?

IN LOVING MEMORY

EULOGY FOR SLAVERY IN THE 21ST CENTURY

Rims shining, diamonds sparkling, money stacking
Dropped out
What is good in the hood?
I'm blowed off that whatever
Cell doors closing, barbed wire fences
Family searched, guards on the perch
Visiting hours are over
Back to the norm, they're all gone
Man up, be strong, or grab your ankles
Loved her so much, had to make her my baby
So full of drama
Was the finest thing on the block
Down broad
She stopped visiting
Now her phone is disconnected
Soon as I hit the pavement
She will love me all over again
And I'll be sure to screw her best friend
Payback, that is
Push-ups, sit-ups
Got to stay in shape
All I'm thinking about is my paper
Ready to get out, I'm smarter now
I've learned new tricks
Baby I'm home
Surprise, surprise
Another man is living in the house I paid for

ISIS M. ELIJAH

Keep it moving
My new baby mama is a down broad
Rims shining, diamonds sparkling, money stacking
I am blowed off that whatever
Learned all new tricks in the pen
So, how did I get another 5 to 10?

WHEN CRAZY MEETS CRAZY

Hey, baby what's your name?
What's your number?
Can we have dinner later?
Will do whatever to get that
Even tell her I love her
Dinner was good
Can I come in?
Stayed until morning
Should be a sin
Thanks for everything, baby
Will call you later
She called me ten times the same day
This is going to get ugly
No, she didn't show up at my house unannounced
Couldn't get to the door before my live-in
"Thought you were single", said the random
I tried to explain to my live-in
"Baby, I don't even know who this person is"
Now all of my tires are slashed
Crazy done met crazy

ISIS M. ELIJAH

SHADE TREE

Hey there
How are you today?
Wanna throw on the shades?
Wanna lie in bed and call off work?
Wanna pull the sheets over your head?
That thing was not yours
That thing was for sale
Had already been bought
Not to the highest bidder
Not this time
The auctioneers divided up the cost
Wholesale stock
Giving the nudge
Not wanting to be bothered
Always spending your money
He never gave out a dime
Be happy he's gone
A total waste of time
Wait a minute
Break
Learn from your mistake
Now, crawl out from under the shade tree

Y'ALL BREAKING MY HEART

Y'all breaking my heart
Selfish
Greedy
Unhappy
Not supportive
Needy
Will settle for anything
Coming up with nothing
Grow up
Clarify
Caught
Crime
Pretending
Arrested
Insecure
Y'all breaking my heart
Calling me at 3 in the morning
What can I do?
I was not there
Stand or fall
Spending lavishly and bouncing checks
Throwing away good money to impress phonies
Your choice
Not mine
You do the crime
You do the time
But you want me to be your knight
Y'all breaking my heart

ISIS M. ELIJAH

SECRET

Was something taken from you?
Were you forced not to tell?
Do you have a secret?
Does it make your teeth clench?
Does it make your jaws tighten?
You might want to cry
You might want to fight
All alone in a room
Tears roll down your face
Heartbroken
Deprived
The pain makes life seem like a waste
Set it free
You have not done anything wrong
Sing a song
If you can't fathom telling a soul
Sing a song
Peace

MOST ENDANGERED SPECIES

BRING IT BACK

It's not your time
Bring it back
No, not suicide
Bring it back
It's not that bad
Bring it back
Scared
Bring it back
Broke
Bring it back
Lapsed on the note
Bring it back
Evacuate the premises
Bring it back
Repossessed the transportation
Bring it back
Left for good
Bring it back
And I live to see another day
Life is good
Life is great
I can make it better
Stabilize, materialize
Positive, definitive choices
Oh my, what is that?
Haven't felt that in a long time
What is it?
My pulse

ISIS M. ELIJAH

DUNG
(AKA DROPPINGS BY TIMOTHY)

Pour scented powder on it
Spray ammonia all over it
Scatter it with dirt and sand
Cover every bit with vanilla and cinnamon
Roll it up in newspaper
Place it in a plastic bag liner
After all of the cover up
Scratch and sniff
What does it smell like?

www.ingramcontent.com/pod-product-compliance
Lightning Source LLC
Chambersburg PA
CBHW021801230426
43669CB00006B/161